TIM FLANNERY

EXPLORING THE INCREDIBLE WORLD IN THE CLOUDS

WEIRD, WILD, AMAZING!

ART BY SAM CALDWELL

SKY

FOR COLEBY AND DANIEL

First published in Australia in 2019 by Hardie Grant Egmont as
part of EXPLORE YOUR WORLD: Weird, Wild, Amazing!
Previously published in the US in 2020 as part of WEIRD, WILD, AMAZING!:
Exploring the Incredible World of Animals.

For information about permission to reproduce selections from this book, write to
Permissions, W. W. Norton & Company, Inc., 500 Fifth Avenue, New York, NY 10110

For information about special discounts for bulk purchases, please contact
W. W. Norton Special Sales at specialsales@wwnorton.com or 800-233-4830

Manufacturing by TransContinental

ISBN 978-1-324-01946-6 (pbk.)

W. W. Norton & Company, Inc., 500 Fifth Avenue, New York, N.Y. 10110
www.wwnorton.com

W. W. Norton & Company Ltd., 15 Carlisle Street, London W1D 3BS

2 4 6 8 0 9 7 5 3 1

TIM FLANNERY

EXPLORING THE INCREDIBLE WORLD IN THE CLOUDS

WEIRD, WILD, AMAZING!

ART BY
SAM CALDWELL

SKY

Norton Young Readers

An Imprint of W. W. Norton & Company
Independent Publishers Since 1923

INTRODUCTION

I've been interested in animals and fossils for as long as I can remember. I grew up in the suburbs of Melbourne, Victoria, Australia, and there weren't a lot of opportunities near my home to see cool creatures. But when I was eight years old, I was walking on a sandbank at low tide and saw a strange rock. It had markings on it, and I suspected it was something special. I took it to the museum, where a man in a white coat brought me to a hall filled with gray steel cabinets. The man opened one, pulled out a drawer, and lifted out a rock identical to mine. "It's *Lovenia forbesi*," he told me, "the fossilized remains of an extinct sea urchin. They are quite common in the rocks near my home." It was, he thought, about 10 million years old. I was awestruck. Then he asked, "Are you interested in dinosaurs?"

could hardly speak. Learning about fossils led to a big breakthrough for me, and in the months and years that followed I would snorkel and scuba-dive in the bay near where I found that first fossilized sea urchin. I remember one winter afternoon, I spied a length of fossil whale jaw, nearly as long as me, lying on the bottom. Another day, I chanced upon the tooth of a megalodon shark lying in the shallows.

The man put the fossilized sea urchin back, closed the drawer, and opened another. "Hold out your hand," he said, as he placed an odd pointed rock on it. "This is the Cape Paterson Claw. It's a claw from the foot of a dinosaur, and it is the only dinosaur bone ever found in Victoria."

I held the Cape Paterson Claw! I was so excited that I

As I grew up, I went further and further afield, into the Australian desert and Great Barrier Reef, where I encountered water-holding frogs, red kangaroos, and magnificent coral. I became a mammologist—someone who studies living mammals. For 20 years I was the curator of mammals at the Australian Museum in Sydney. I visited most of the islands between eastern Indonesia and Fiji, discovering new species of marsupials, rats, and bats. By the time I left the job I'd been on 26 expeditions into the islands north of Australia and discovered more than 30 new living mammal species.

I WAS MORE THAN INTERESTED.
I WAS OBSESSED.

If you're interested in animals and nature, you can volunteer at a museum or on a dig, participate in a citizen science program like the Great Backyard Bird Count, or just start your own studies in a local tide pool or pond. If you decide to do a study by yourself, you need to take careful notes and send them to an expert in a museum or university to check them.

If you don't live near a beach, you can study nature in a local park or backyard. The soil and plants will be filled with living things, including birds and insects. But be sure to stay safe as you investigate!

If you're interested in fossils, keep your eyes on the rocks. Look out for curious shapes. And if you do find something, photograph it, or if it is small and portable, take it to your local museum. Most have services to help identify it.

When I was very young I often wished that I had a fun book that would tell me about the weirdest creatures on Earth. That's what I've tried to create here, for you. I hope that you find reading it to be a great adventure in itself, and that it leaves you wanting to see more of the wonderful and mysterious world around us.

Tim Flannery

CONCEPTS

CLIMATE CHANGE

Earth's climate is changing because of pollution that humans are putting into the atmosphere. Greenhouse gases like carbon dioxide from burning coal, gas, and oil are causing the ground, oceans, and atmosphere to warm up. This might sound good if you live in a cold place, but many consequences of the warming are bad for living things. For example, warmer conditions mean that less water is available in some places, and creatures living in the warming oceans often have less food and oxygen. As seas rise and rainfall changes, and the atmosphere warms, entire habitats are disappearing, causing species to become threatened or even extinct.

SO SAD.

EVOLUTION

Evolution is a word that describes how animals and plants change over generations. Each generation of living things is made up of individuals that differ a little from each other: some might be bigger, or more brightly colored, for example. And in nature, more animals are born (or germinate, if they're plants) than the environment can support. This means that the individuals that do best in their environment are most likely to survive. For example, if bigger, brighter animals or plants survive better, with each new generation the population will be made up of bigger, brighter individuals. Over many generations, the changes brought about by this "natural selection" can be so great that new species are created.

HABITATS

Habitats include places on land, in water, and even in the air. They are the places where animals live, and they vary greatly all across the world. Deserts are very dry habitats, tundras are very cold ones, while rainforests are very stable ones (with little temperature change, for example, between winter and summer). As animals and plants evolve, they become better adapted to their particular habitat. In the *Weird, Wild, Amazing!* books, habitats are grouped into four very broad categories: water, sky, forest, and desert/grasslands. Within each there are many different habitats—far too many to list.

FOSSILS

Fossils are the remains of plants and animals that lived in the past. The chances of you, or any living thing, becoming a fossil is very small. Maybe one in a billion! The first step toward a fossil being created happens when the remains of a plant or animal are buried in sediment like sand or mud. If the conditions are right, over thousands of years the sediment turns to rock, and the remains become "petrified" (which means turned to rock) or preserved in some other form, like an impression (such as a footprint).

COMMON NAMES v. SCIENTIFIC NAMES

Animals and plants have two kinds of names: a common name and a scientific name. The common name of a species is the name that you generally know them by, and these names can vary in different areas. For example, "wolf" is a common name in English, but wolves are called "lobo" in Spanish, and have many different names in other languages. But the scientific name never varies. This means that by using the scientific name, an English-speaking scientist and a Spanish-speaking scientist can understand each other.

Scientific names have two parts. For wolves, the scientific name is *Canis lupus*. The first part (*Canis*, in this case) is known as the genus name, and it is shared with close relatives. For example, the golden jackal's scientific name—*Canis aureus*—also begins with *Canis*. But the combination of genus and species name is unique. For wolves, the species name (*lupus*) means "wolf" in Latin.

EXTINCTION

Scientists use terms like "vulnerable," "threatened," and "endangered" to describe how likely an organism is to become extinct. Extinction occurs when the last individual of a species dies. If an animal is endangered, it means that very few individuals exist, and that they might soon become extinct. If an animal is threatened, it means that they are likely to become endangered in the future, while an animal being classed as vulnerable means that they are likely to become threatened.

ANIMAL TYPES

Animals and plants are classified according to their evolution. Animals, for example, can be divided into those with backbones (vertebrates) and those without (invertebrates). You can't always tell which group a plant or animal belongs to by just looking at them. Sometimes looks can be misleading! Falcons are related not to eagles or kites, which they resemble, but parrots. Parrots and falcons are classified in a group called "Austroaves," meaning "southern birds," because they originated in the southern hemisphere.

CONSERVATION

Conservation means taking care of nature and all of its plants and animals. Governments help by creating national parks, and fining litterbugs and polluters. Scientists play an important role in conservation by studying how we can help various species. You can be a conservationist in your own backyard: just plant a native tree that will become a home to the birds.

CONSERVE TO PRESERVE!

ALBATROSSES

The albatross is a type of seabird that spends most of its time flying over the ocean, a really long way from land. From a distance, you might think albatrosses don't look all that different from seagulls. You'd be wrong, though! For starters, albatrosses are huge. As in, bigger-than-you huge. They can also dive deep underwater to catch their prey, fly ridiculously long distances and make some seriously weird sounds. And wait until you find out where they sleep!

WHERE CAN I SEE AN ALBATROSS?

Most of them inhabit the great Southern Ocean, but a few types also live around the North Pacific Ocean.

A GROUP OF ALBATROSSES IS CALLED A FLOCK, A ROOKERY, A WEIGHT, OR A GAM.

GLOBE-TROTTING BIRDS

Albatrosses travel for most of their long lives. Some birds are still gliding around when they're 60! The average albatross will travel more than 4.3 million miles in a lifetime —enough to circle the world about 180 times, or make more than six round trips to the moon.

SALTY SEA WATER

Because they spend most of their time over the ocean, it's tricky for albatrosses to find fresh water—so they have to drink sea water. Drinking sea water is TERRIBLE for humans—we get even thirstier and start to hallucinate when we do it—but albatrosses have a nifty system to deal with all that salt. They have a special passage above their beak that leaks out the salt that builds up in their blood.

CLIMATE CHANGE

Declining fish populations mean that there is less food available for albatrosses, and rising sea levels make it harder for them to build nests in some of their usual places.

MOO!

?

A DATE WITH AN ALBATROSS

Albatrosses date for a really long time before settling down to have a family—sometimes more than two years! During this time they dance for each other, groom each other, and make all kinds of bizarre sounds to impress each other, including one that makes them sound like a cow.

Albatrosses gobble down a surprising variety of foods—almost anything they can fit down their gullets. They love squid, and they have more than one way of catching them.

▶ Albatrosses can spend hours paddling around in circles in the middle of the ocean. This looks innocent, but is actually a sneaky albatross trap! It's thought that this odd behavior stirs up bioluminescent creatures, which in turn attract squid to the surface of the water, where the albatross can catch them.

▶ Albatrosses don't have to wait for squid to come to the surface—they can dive 41 feet underwater to chase their prey! Squid don't make it easy for albatrosses to catch them, but it's tricky to avoid a bird that can dive with the speed and precision of an albatross.

▶ It's easiest to scavenge for dead squid because they float toward the surface of the water, where the albatross scoops them up using its large beak. And, of course, dead squid don't try to escape!

HOW BIG IS AN ALBATROSS?

All albatrosses are large, but the biggest of all is **the wandering albatross**. It's a true giant, weighing up to 26.5 pounds—twice as big as a bald eagle. It also has a 11.2-foot wingspan, the largest of any bird. Your bed probably isn't even 7 feet from top to bottom, which gives you an idea of how huge these birds really are!

SHARKS ALIVE

A young albatross's first flight is brief, typically involving a splashdown in the sea near its nest. Huge tiger sharks often lie in wait in these areas, but the albatross babies are so excited about being out of the nest that they're oblivious to the danger. They bob about in the shallows, casually staring down the advancing sharks or even giving them a cheeky peck on the snout as they plough past. But it doesn't take too long for the young birds to catch on to the danger lurking below. After all, the birds that don't learn fast are likely to become a shark's snack!

SUPER PARENTS

When they have a baby, albatross parents don't have time for anything but taking care of their chick. They take it in turns to leave their cliff-top nest to find food, and often travel more than 600 miles for a single chick-sized meal! They don't carry food all that way back in their beaks, either—they swallow it and then vomit it up for their chick to eat. Gross! With all that travelling, albatross parents hardly ever see each other. They usually only have a few seconds to catch up in between one bird arriving home and the other one setting off. It makes sense that albatross pairs only have one baby at a time. Raising an albatross chick is hard work!

ALBATROSSES DON'T SLEEPWALK, THEY SLEEP*FLY*

Albatrosses spend more of their lives aloft than almost any other kind of bird. They don't have big enough chest muscles to fly by flapping their wings. Instead, they stretch out their huge, heavy wings and cleverly use the wind to glide through the air, a bit like how a human uses a hang-glider. They can't fly if there isn't any wind. Flapping to take off is hard, but once they're up in the sky they can relax and let the wind carry them. Some albatrosses stay in the air close to 24/7 for the first six years of their lives, only stopping occasionally to rest on the ocean surface. That doesn't mean they stay awake for six years straight, though—they just sleep as they fly! We know this because a dozing bird occasionally flies into a boat—talk about a wake-up call!

BIRDS IN PERIL

Many species of albatross are critically endangered. The main threats to their health are fishing hooks and plastic waste. When they try to eat bait from fishing lines hanging off the sides of boats, they can get stuck on the hook and dragged underwater. The birds can confuse plastic waste with food, and when they eat it the plastic fills their stomach so they can't fit any real food in. So make sure you never litter—your waste could end up in the ocean, where an albatross could eat it.

5

BATS

There are about 1,300 different types of bat, and they're the second most abundant mammal in the world after rodents. Rodents might come out on top when it comes to sheer quantity, but bats are the clear winner in other categories—they're the only mammal that can fly! The stories about bats sucking blood like vampires are true, but not all bats are scary—some bats are adorable little bundles of fluff, and others use their moose-like noses to make hilarious honking sounds. They're very versatile!

WHERE CAN I SEE A BAT?

Bats live in most parts of the world, but they prefer places that are warmer. You won't find them in Antarctica or the Arctic—too cold!

A NEED FOR SPEED

Brazilian free-tailed bats can fly up to 100 miles per hour.

A GROUP OF BATS IS CALLED A COLONY OR A CLOUD.

VAMPIRE BATS

Yes, **vampire bats** are real—but don't worry, you're unlikely to get bitten by one because they prefer the blood of animals like horses and cows. The good news is that the prey of a vampire bat usually survives the attack, just with less blood!

▶ Because blood is mostly made of water, vampire bats need to eat every night to get enough nutrition. They can skip one meal if they absolutely have to, but if they skip more than that they won't survive.

▶ Vampire bats don't catch their prey by swooping in from the air—they approach on the ground, sometimes running along on all fours to chase their dinner.

▶ Vampire bats have sharp fangs that they use to slice into the veins of their prey. Blood is designed to thicken when you're injured so that your wounds can heal over, but vampire bats have a special kind of saliva that stops the blood from thickening while they're eating. **INGENIOUS!**

▶ Vampire bats have built-in infrared vision, so they can see their prey moving in the dark by sensing the heat of their bodies.

▶ Vampire bats are really generous. They share their meals with other vampire bats, but the way they do it is pretty gross. They vomit up the blood that they just ate so that their friend can eat it!

BLIND ~ AS A ~ BAT

You might have heard the expression "blind as a bat," but a bat's eyesight can be three times better than the average human's. And their hearing abilities are even more incredible! Bats make sounds that echo back in different ways depending on what is nearby. These complex call and echo patterns allow bats to create a highly detailed map of their surroundings. The sounds they make can be incredibly loud, but you can't hear them because they're at a pitch that human ears can't pick up.

BURROWING BATS

Bats don't just fly and walk on the ground—some of them dig under the ground, too! These burrowing bats live in New Zealand and are able to fold up their wings so that they can dig through rotting trees and under the earth.

In 1991 I discovered a kind of bat that was thought to have been extinct since the Ice Age. **Bulmer's fruit bat** is the world's largest cave-dwelling bat, with a wingspan of about 3 feet. The bats once lived all over Papua New Guinea, but by the time I found them they only lived in a single cave. The cave was a vertical shaft about half a mile deep, and a few survivors of human hunting had found a refuge there. To confirm what I'd discovered, I had to climb up a tree hanging over the cave at night and set a net. It was very scary!

I once discovered a new species of flying fox on New Ireland in Papua New Guinea. When I was searching for bats I had to climb a mountain of bat poo and wade through a lake of bat pee inside a huge cave. The bat that I discovered is called **Ennis' flying fox**. Its wings look like dead banana leaves, and by day it hangs in banana plants and other trees.

THE BAT CAVE

The biggest bat colony is in a cave in Texas— about 20 million **free-tailed bats** live there. They sleep inside the cave during the day and flood out at night to feed on insects, filling the sky with a swirling black mass of wings.

BABY BATS

Dyak fruit bats are one of the very few animal species whose dads produce milk to help feed their young.

FOXES AND BUMBLEBEES

Flying foxes are the biggest bats in the world. Despite their name, they're not related to foxes—they just have a foxy-looking face. They're a type of fruit bat and can have a wingspan of close to 6 feet. Even though these bats are very large, they don't weigh much—the largest ones only weigh about 3 pounds, which is the same as half a brick. That's one of the reasons they can hang upside down without feeling ill—they're too light to have the same "blood rush to the head" feeling that we do after hanging upside down for too long.

The smallest bat in the world is the **bumblebee bat**. It isn't only the smallest type of bat, though—it's also the smallest mammal in the world! It weighs less than a tenth of an ounce, which means two of these bats put together still weigh less than an average piece of letter paper. They're usually about 1 inch long, which is a little shorter than a paperclip.

THE PERFECT NAME

▶ The **Yoda bat** has big green-and-yellow-tinged ears that stick out to the side and a wide mouth stretched into a gentle smile. Many people think this type of bat looks particularly wise and kind, like a certain small Jedi.

▶ **Leaf-nosed bats** have large, oddly shaped noses. The shape of their noses varies, but it often looks like some kind of crinkled leaf has fallen from a tree and landed on the bat's face.

▶ **Spear-nosed bats** have a large, fleshy spike protruding above their pig-like noses.

▶ Most bats have pretty sizeable ears, so you know the **big-eared bat** must have REALLY big ones to earn its name. These bats have tiny faces that are dwarfed by the long rabbit-like ears that stick straight up from their heads.

▶ **Clear-winged woolly bats** have a particularly soft, fuzzy body and, unsurprisingly, see-through wings!

▶ The average **wrinkle-faced bat** probably has more wrinkles than your grandparents. These bats have masses of grooves in the bare, pink skin of their faces, as well as flaps and folds of loose skin.

CLIMATE CHANGE

Increasing temperatures are difficult for bats to deal with. In Australia, soaring summer temperatures can cause large numbers of bats to die from overheating and dehydration.

THE CUTEST BAT IN THE WORLD

The **Honduran white bat** is tiny, with fluffy white fur. Its ears, nose, feet and parts of its wings are bright yellow and orange, and its ears are shaped like little leaves.

These bats love to go camping, and make their own tents by slicing the large leaves of tropical plants so that flaps fold down on both sides to create a cozy green shelter. These tents help keep the bats hidden from predators and protect them from the weather.

CUTE!

CLEVER!

MOTHS

Is a moth just a less exciting version of a butterfly? Absolutely not! In fact, some moths are so ridiculously beautiful that spiders take one look at them and let them go instead of eating them (there's a bit more to that story, but we'll get to that later). They love pretending to be things they're not, like hornets or eyeballs or lumps of poop. Speaking of poop—the way they go to the toilet is like nothing you've ever heard of. They also love to eat nectar and honey and other sweet things (except for the ones that have more . . . Transylvanian tastes).

MOTHS AND BUTTERFLIES

Moths are closely related to butterflies, as they evolved from the same ancestor about 250 million years ago. Moths are far more common than butterflies—there are around ten moths to every single butterfly in the world.

A GROUP OF MOTHS IS SOMETIMES CALLED A WHISPER.

WHERE CAN I SEE A MOTH?

Moths live all over the world.

WHAT'S THE DEAL WITH MOTH MOUTHS?

Moths generally eat a lot more when they're caterpillars because they're building up energy to transform into moths. Moths and caterpillars eat different kinds of food, too.

100% BIRD TEARS

▶ Caterpillars particularly enjoy eating plants. Sometimes a moth's name gives you a clue about its favorite thing to nibble on when it's a caterpillar, such as the **cherry dagger moth** or **oak moth**, which feed on cherry trees and oak trees respectively.

▶ Once caterpillars turn into moths they generally lose their chewing mouths and develop a long, thin proboscis, which they use like a straw to suck up liquid foods like plant nectar. Some moths keep their mouths and continue eating firmer parts of plants such as pollen.

▶ Some moths don't have mouths or proboscises at all, so they can't eat anything once they've developed beyond their caterpillar stage. They have to eat a lot as caterpillars so that they get all the nutrients they need to last them through their short lives as moths.

▶ Moths with a long proboscis, such as the **hummingbird moth**, drink plant nectar from mid-air. They hover above a flower and let their proboscis uncurl down into the middle of the flower where the nectar is stored. **Darwin's hawkmoth** has a proboscis that can be longer than a ruler, which allows it to reach inside the particularly deep tropical flowers.

▶ A blood-sucking **vampire moth** that lives in Siberia pushes its proboscis, which is covered in tiny spikes and barbs, under the skin of animals to reach the blood flowing underneath.

▶ Some moths use their proboscis to spear through the eyelids of sleeping birds to reach the salt-rich stores of tears in their eyes. The proboscis is so thin that it doesn't hurt the birds—they can sleep right through it!

FLANNERY FILE

I was exploring high in the mountains of Papua New Guinea, and one drizzly night I visited a friend living in a nearby village. He lit a lamp when I arrived and as we sat and talked, moths became attracted to the light. Tens of thousands of them flew through the window and filled the hut! They were all different varieties—some were the size of a steering wheel, and others were as tiny as the nail on my pinkie finger. Eventually we could hardly see each other because there were so many moths fluttering through the air between us. It was a very hot night, so we were sweating quite a bit, and the moths were landing all over us to drink our sweat. It was an incredible sight!

AN ORNATE MOTH

HONEY RAIDER

Ornate moth caterpillars eat the rattlepod bush, a plant that produces a toxin that's meant to deter things from eating its leaves. Ornate moth caterpillars are one of the very few things that are immune to the toxins. These tough little bugs actually store the poison in their bodies to use themselves! After the caterpillar has transformed into a moth, it releases frothy, poison-laden blood from near the base of its wings. The poison is so lethal that predators have learned to recognize and fear the markings of this moth. For example, if an ornate moth is caught in a spiderweb, the spider will often carefully cut it free instead of trying to eat it. Interestingly, the poison isn't just used against predators. Males of the species rely on their toxins to attract a mate—if they're poison-free, female moths are not interested in them.

Death's-head hawkmoths, named after the distinctive skull-like markings on their backs, love eating honey—so they have developed several techniques to steal it from inside beehives. They make a loud screeching noise using an accordion-like action that confuses the bees. They are also able to produce a chemical that mimics the smell of bees, which helps them sneak into hives without being discovered. Finally, they have a partial immunity to bee venom, so if they only get a couple of stings as they're charging into the hive they might still make it out alive. Imagine risking your life every time you wanted a meal!

HOW BIG IS A MOTH?

Moths can be anywhere from as small as a period to as large as a dinner plate. **Atlas moths** are one of the largest in the world, with wingspans that can be as long as a ruler. The smallest moths, known as **pygmy moths**, have tiny bodies and wingspans of just one tenth of an inch. Those particular moths live all over the world, but they're so small that they're easy to miss.

CAMOUFLAGE OR COSTUME?

Many moths have intricate patterns and vivid colors on their wings that frighten predators, who know that these markers are indicators of toxicity. But it is not just poisonous moths that look this way—some harmless species imitate their intricate colors. These trickster moths evolved from more camouflaged species that gave up their protective coloring for a different kind of protection.

▶ The **buff-tip moth** curls its mottled brown wings into a tube shape when it sits on branches so that it looks just like a broken-off twig.

▶ The **hornet moth** has hornet-like coloring as well as a similar body shape and completely clear wings. These moths also copy a hornet's style of flight, making every effort to convince predators that they are not defenseless moths but hornets with a powerful sting.

▶ Some moths and caterpillars, including the caterpillars of some **hawkmoths**, have patterns on them that look like large eyes.

▶ The **pearly wood-nymph moth** looks just like a blob of bird poo! EW!

PINEAPPLE PERFUME

WHEN THEY'RE LOOKING FOR A MATE, MALE GOLD SWIFT MOTHS WILL RELEASE A SCENT THAT IS IRRESISTIBLE TO FEMALE MOTHS—THE SMELL OF RIPE PINEAPPLE!

HOW DO MOTHS GO TO THE TOILET?

Many moths, including **Gluphisia moths**, like to congregate around puddles and gulp down vast amounts of water. They're too small to need all that water to hydrate, so why do they drink so much? Well, there are small amounts of salt in the water, which is good for moths. They strip the salt out of the water as they drink, then get rid of the excess water—by shooting it out of their butts! They can squirt out around 20 of these powerful streams every minute as they drink—and each stream can be 1 foot long! This whole process has its own special name—it's called "puddling."

VULTURES

S
K
Y

•

V
U
L
T
U
R
E
S

With their gloomy looks and strange, often bald heads, vultures seem pretty ominous—especially when they gather around injured animals, waiting for them to die so they can have a feed. But these meat-eating birds don't deserve their bad reputation—they rarely kill other animals, preferring to eat those that have recently died. They're basically tidying up gross messes as they eat, making them some of the most helpful birds on the planet.

A GROUP OF VULTURES IS CALLED A VENUE OR A COMMITTEE IF THEY'RE ON THE GROUND, BUT IF THEY'RE FLYING, THEY'RE CALLED A KETTLE. SOMETIMES A GROUP OF FEEDING VULTURES IS CALLED A WAKE.

WHERE CAN I SEE A VULTURE?

Old World vultures live in Asia, Africa, and Europe; the New World vultures live in the Americas. Between the different species, vultures live on every continent except Australia and Antarctica.

WHAT DOES A VULTURE SOUND LIKE?

Vultures aren't all that noisy. New World vultures don't even have vocal organs! Instead of singing or calling, these birds are more likely to grunt or even hiss as a way of communicating.

WOULD YOU EAT WHAT A VULTURE EATS?

Vultures generally eat animals that are already dead, including carrion, which is animals that have started to rot. But they prefer their meals to be fresh—animals that have recently died are ideal. Vultures will occasionally go after live prey, but in those cases the animal is already injured or weakened in some way. Animals such as zebras, wildebeest, elephants, hippos, and antelope are all common meals, but sometimes vultures eat things that are a little more surprising.

▶ Although meat is by far their most common food, vultures do eat some plant matter, including things like rotting fruits.

▶ **Palm-nut vultures** are almost entirely vegetarian! They eat some small animals, such as frogs and fish, but mostly large quantities of fruit from palm trees.

▶ **Egyptian vultures** have been known to use stones to break open the eggs of large birds, such as ostriches, then eat the gloopy insides.

▶ **Bearded vultures** mostly eat bones! They drop them from high up in the sky to smash on rocky areas below. Once the bones have shattered, which can take a few tries, the birds guzzle down the bone marrow, as well as shards of actual bone. They also use this trick to break open the shells of turtles so that they can get at the flesh inside.

FEEDING FRENZY!

Sometimes hundreds of vultures will feed on the same dead animal, especially one that is particularly large. With so many birds feeding at once, mealtimes can get pretty hectic. The birds flap around in a frenzy, pecking and stepping on each other to get at the food. Unsurprisingly, bigger vultures have the most success in a situation like this, with smaller and younger birds often forced to wait until the end to feed on the scraps.

A group of vultures can eat a carcass down to the bone in a matter of minutes. They tear off chunks of food and stuff them into a pouch in their neck called a "crop." Only after they've packed the crop full of food will they sit still and actually digest their meal. If they have chicks, they won't digest the food at all—they'll fly back to their nest and regurgitate the food for the chicks to eat.

STARTING A FAMILY

Different vulture species nest in different ways—Old World vultures build large nests made from sticks, usually in trees or on cliffs, while New World vultures generally nest in bare holes dug in the ground, known as "scrapes." Some nests, particularly ones belonging to Old World vultures, are even bigger than queen-sized beds! Vulture eggs can be quite beautiful, and are often covered in brown or purple speckles. The chicks hatch with large feet and bare beaks poking out from the fluffy white down that covers their bodies. They look almost cuddly, but also very odd!

WEAPONIZED VOMIT

Some vultures, like **turkey vultures**, have highly acidic vomit, so if they throw up on the sensitive parts of a predator, it can actually hurt them. It also smells really, really bad! This isn't surprising, as its main ingredient is rotting, half-digested lumps of meat. There's another reason vultures throw up when they're threatened—puking up a large meal makes the birds considerably lighter, so they can make a quick escape by taking flight.

TOXIC WASTE

UNDER THREAT

As large animals such as elephants become less common, vultures will struggle to find food. Populations of these large birds are declining very quickly, partly due to a lack of food, but also because they are often hunted or poisoned by humans.

WHO'S WHO

There are three groups of vultures, all of which descended from different birds of prey. The first two groups, both known as Old World vultures, contain a total of 18 species. They find their food using their keen eyesight—they have a terrible sense of smell.

The third group is called the New World vultures. Some New World vultures, such as **turkey vultures**, have an excellent sense of smell. The part of their brain that processes scents is extra-large, helping them to find carcasses that are below the tree cover and not visible from the air.

WHAT'S THE DEAL WITH

Vultures regularly poo and pee on their legs, and they do it on purpose. There are two very good reasons for doing something so disgusting. First, it helps them to cool down, a bit like tipping a glass of water over your feet—only a whole lot ickier. Their poo and pee also have a lot of something called uric acid in them, which helps kill any bacteria they might have picked up by traipsing around in dead bodies.

Egyptian vultures eat cow poo, and they especially love the yellow kind. The yellower the poo is, the more nutrients it has in it—plus it helps keep their faces a vivid yellow, which helps them find mates and intimidate other vultures.

HOW HIGH CAN THEY FLY?

A **Rüppell's griffon vulture** has been seen flying close to 7 miles above the ground, making it one of the highest-flying birds in the world—if not the highest.

PESTS OR HEROES?

Vultures have really strong stomach acids, which is how they're able to eat flesh that has sometimes already started rotting and could be carrying various infections or disease. They can even break down anthrax bacteria, which would kill you! By eating the bodies of dead and decaying animals, vultures are often helping to stop the spread of lethal bacteria. They might look creepy, and their diet might gross you out, but these birds are definitely your friends!

SERIOUSLY BIG BIRDS

The **Andean condors** are the biggest vultures. They can weigh up to 33 pounds, about the same as a large toddler. They also grow to 4 feet tall, which is more like the height of a seven-year-old child. Not bad for a bird! Their wingspan can extend to 11.5 feet, and they have the largest wing area of any bird in the world.

HOATZINS

Despite what they look or act like, hoatzins aren't an odd combination of bird and lizard, or bird and cow. They're the only survivor of a very ancient line of birds, which is part of the reason they look quite different from every other bird species. With their vivid blue faces, bright red eyes, and long, feathery crests, hoatzins are impossible to miss—especially when gathered in groups of 100, which can happen. And their appearance isn't even the weirdest thing about them . . .

HOW BIG IS A HOATZIN?

Adult hoatzins are about 2 feet tall, which means three of them stacked up would be as long as your bed. They're not heavy, though—even fully grown they weigh a little less than 2 pounds.

TAKE TO THE SKY! OR NOT . . .

Adult hoatzins can fly, but not very well. You're more likely to spot them perched in a tree doing their favorite thing (eating), or digesting.

WHERE CAN I SEE A HOATZIN?

Hoatzins live in South America, especially around the Amazon and Orinoco river basins.

GRAZING ANIMALS

Hoatzins are herbivores. Their favorite foods are fresh leaves and buds—the younger and tenderer, the better. Many birds have a crop, which is a pouch in their throat used to store and digest food, but hoatzins' crops are unusual in a couple of ways. For a start, they're extremely large. They also have special ridges inside them that help grind and shred food after it is swallowed. Once the food has been broken up, hoatzins use a special mix of bacteria to ferment their food so that it can be fully digested. They are the only birds in the world that digest food in this way—other animals with similar systems are cows and sheep.

TERRIBLE AT SNEAKING

Whether they're flying or clambering through trees with their strong feet, hoatzins aren't exactly graceful. They're loud and clumsy as a general rule, so it's lucky they don't have to sneak up on their food. Aside from the noise they make crashing around through the trees or undergrowth, hoatzins also make a wide variety of hissing, grunting, wheezing, croaking, and rasping sounds. No cute little tweets here!

NOT YOUR AVERAGE BABY

Hoatzins like to build their nests on branches that hang out over water. That way, if a predator is approaching, their chicks—who are unable to fly—can escape by tumbling out into the water below. Plunging into a river might sound worse than taking a chance in the nest, but hoatzin chicks aren't your average baby birds! They can swim quite well and, as long as they don't get snapped up by a passing crocodile, they are able to paddle to shore and climb back up into the nest. Yes, you read that right— the chicks CLIMB back into the nest, using their claws. As if that's not weird enough, their claws aren't even on their feet—they're on their wings. Hoatzin chicks have two big, sharp claws on each wing, which means they can grasp onto branches and climb around until they're old enough to fly. When that time comes, usually a week or so after hatching, the claws simply fall off.

STINKING IT UP

Hoatzins are often called "stink birds" or "skunk birds" and, to be honest, they deserve the name. They smell terrible! Some people describe their stench as being similar to cow manure. The smell comes from the special way they digest their meals. As their food ferments it releases a smelly gas called methane. The birds then burp the gas out, sharing the pungent side effects of their digestion process with the world around them.

GROSS!

BURRRP!!

EAGLES

There are many different species of eagle, some more closely related than others, and they're also related to other large birds of prey, such as hawks and kites. Eagles are particularly huge, with hooked beaks, enormous wings, and powerful talons—they cut quite an impressive figure. Eagles are known as fierce hunters, elegant flyers, and intimidatingly regal birds. Which is all true! But they can also be awkward (just look at one trying to swim) and are surprisingly likely to steal their dinner rather than hunt for it themselves.

WHERE CAN I SEE AN EAGLE?

Eagles live in Africa, Eurasia, across the Americas, and in Australia.

A MISLEADING NAME

Bald eagles aren't bald, but because the feathers on their bodies are dark brown and the ones on their heads are white they do look a bit like they're featherless on top—especially from a distance.

A GROUP OF EAGLES IS CALLED A CONVOCATION OR AN AERIE.

WHAT DOES AN EAGLE EAT?

Each species of eagle has its own favorite food, with common snacks including rodents, fish, reptiles, insects, and other birds. But they also eat things that are a lot more surprising! Turtles, small kangaroos, mountain goats, sloths, deer, flamingos, wallabies, and even small crocodiles are on the menu for some eagles.

Eagles eat every part of their prey—they're not picky. They have strong stomach acid that helps them break down their food, even the bones! The few bits and pieces that can't be easily digested, such as feathers, are coughed up as pellets that look a bit like chunks of poop. **YUCK!**

A BIRD'S-EYE VIEW

Eagles have excellent eyesight, about four or five times better than yours. They can see prey from over 2 miles away.

HOW BIG IS AN EAGLE?

The impressive size of an eagle is perhaps best seen in flight, when their unfurled wings are on show. Some of the biggest wingspans can stretch up to 8 feet across, such as on the **Steller's sea eagle** and the **white-tailed eagle**. The tallest basketball players in history don't measure up to that! Despite this immense size, even the heaviest of the eagles are not particularly weighty—the **Philippine eagle** and Steller's sea eagle are toward the top of the spectrum and still only reach a maximum of 18 to 20 pounds. That's about the same weight as a small beagle.

CALL OF THE WILD

Some eagles, such as **sea eagles**, have calls that are strong and loud. Others, like the **bald eagle**, have much less awe-inspiring calls. Sometimes, when you hear an eagle on TV, its call has actually been enhanced to sound more impressive. **SNEAKY!**

EAGLES ARE CARNIVORES AND APEX PREDATORS, SOMETIMES KILLING ANIMALS MORE THAN FIVE TIMES BIGGER THAN THEM.

▶ Despite having a lethal-looking beak, eagles generally use their talons to catch their prey. The **harpy eagle** has claws at the back of its talons that can rival those of a bear in terms of size, and its legs can be nearly as thick as your ankle.

▶ Hunting often starts in treetop perches, where eagles sit silently and look out for prey moving below, swooping down to pounce on anything that catches their eye. Eagles also dive onto their meals from flight, and they occasionally even run after **YES, SERIOUSLY!** them on foot.

▶ Unlike you, eagles have the ability to see ultraviolet light, which helps them track their prey. All they have to do is follow the trails of pee left by animals marking their territory—the urine reflects ultraviolet light!

▶ Fish eaters, like the **bald eagle** and **African fish eagle**, snatch many of their meals straight out of the water. If their prey is heavy, they'll cling on to it with their talons and drag it toward land. Sometimes they'll even get into the water themselves, keeping a firm grasp on their dinner with their feet and using their

wings like oars to paddle toward solid ground.

▶ Eagles often steal food from smaller birds and will even fight other eagles for food—especially in winter, when meals are scarce. A bald eagle was once caught on camera stealing a dead rabbit from a fox. The young fox wasn't giving up without a fight and was lifted into the air by the eagle as they tussled over the meal. Eventually the fox dropped back to the ground and trotted off as the victorious eagle flew off with its stolen dinner. **SHAMELESS!**

A BIG NEST FOR A BIG BIRD

Eagle nests are called "eyries," and they're huge! They're generally built in trees or on cliffs. Eagles use sticks for the base of their nests, and line the inside with grass, feathers, and moss to soften them. **Bald eagle** nests are particularly huge—they can be over 20 feet deep, so an average human adult standing inside wouldn't be able to see over the edge. They can also be over 10 feet wide and weigh over 4,400 pounds. That's heavier than a car!

ANCIENT GIANT

Haast's eagle is now extinct, but it was once the largest eagle in the world. It weighed close to 40 pounds and had a wingspan of 10 feet! This giant bird of prey lived in New Zealand, where it hunted giant flightless birds called moa.

• FLANNERY FILE •

Australian **sea eagles** mate for life. But first they test out the strength of a potential mate in an aerial battle, during which they lock talons and spiral downward through the air. I once saw a pair that were so evenly matched, they stayed locked until they hit the sea more than half a mile from shore. It was a windy day and they were exhausted, waterlogged, yet still fighting in the water! Overhead, a whistling kite circled, tight and low, waiting for one to die!

I set out in my dinghy armed with a yard broom. The kite flew off and the eagles separated. The smaller male had a gash on his breast—a spot of red on otherwise spotless white. I placed the broom under the larger female and she stood steadily on it, entirely unafraid, as I lifted her above head height. She took off, swooping so low over the water I feared she might go in again. Her yellow eyes, with their fearless, imperious gaze, were unforgettable—as was her fearsome beak! The wounded male was younger and more fearful. He kept swimming feebly away from me, but after a dozen attempts he gave up and I swept him into the boat, where he lay with wings hanging over the sides, his head drooping, utterly exhausted. I put him ashore on a rock, where he sat for hours before moving off. I often wonder if they stayed together.

SOARING AND DIVING

Instead of burning through energy by flapping their huge wings, eagles prefer to use warm currents of air to glide through the sky.

▶ Eagles can stay aloft for hours at a time and have been known to reach heights of 10,000 feet as they fly.

▶ Reaching speeds of nearly 30 miles per hour is not uncommon for flying eagles, and they can go even faster when they dive— some, like the **golden eagle**, can reach speeds of more than 120 miles per hour as they plummet toward the earth.

▶ If a **bald eagle** loses a feather from its wing, another feather will fall out from the same area on the other wing so that the eagle can stay balanced as it flies.

CRANES

Cranes are one of the world's oldest surviving bird groups. There are 15 different species of crane, and they're all very social. Large herds of them are often seen gathered near water, causing a ruckus as they call out to each other and take part in flamboyant dancing. Once you find out more about these incredible birds you might become a craniac—the name given to crane-obsessed humans!

LUMPS AND BUMPS

Cranes have incredibly long legs, but not everything is as it seems. Cranes' knobbly "knees" are really the heels of their feet. That means that their "feet" are actually their toes, so cranes don't actually walk—they tiptoe.

WHERE CAN I SEE A CRANE?

Cranes can be found in every part of the world except South America and Antarctica.

A GROUP OF CRANES iS CALLED A HERD, A SEDGE, OR SOMETiMES EVEN A DANCE.

CLIMATE CHANGE

Many cranes make their homes in wetlands—the perfect habitat for finding food and laying eggs. As the planet warms, the wetland homes of cranes are drying out and making it harder for cranes to thrive.

GETTING ROWDY

CRANES SEEM ALMOST IMPOSSIBLY GRACEFUL AS THEY SOAR THROUGH THE SKY OR STEP GENTLY ACROSS MARSHY GROUND. BUT THE NOISES THEY MAKE ARE ANYTHING BUT DELICATE!

HONK!

- **Gray crowned cranes** make a honking sound, and the bright red gular pouch under their beaks can inflate to help make their calls extra loud.

- **Sandhill cranes** have a raucous, rattling call that can travel over 1 mile.

- Pairs of mating cranes sing loud duets during breeding season.

- A crane's windpipe gets longer and longer as the bird matures. By the time it's an adult, the windpipe is far too long to just go straight up and down—it has to curl around like a complex brass instrument instead. The **whooping crane** has the longest windpipe—laid out flat, it would be 5 feet long.

TALL AND LEAN

Sarus cranes are the tallest flying bird in the world, stretching to 6 feet tall—taller than many adult humans. That's nothing compared with the length of their wingspan, though, which is well over 8 feet! These slender birds aren't the heaviest cranes—that title goes to the **red-crowned cranes**, which weigh up to 26 pounds.

STARTING A FAMILY

- Cranes usually mate for life, but if things aren't going well for a pair they sometimes "divorce" and find new mates.

- Their eggs are about 4 inches long, and when the chicks hatch they're about the size of a large apple. They don't stay that small for long, though! Crane chicks grow at an extraordinary rate, sometimes shooting up more than 5 feet in just a few months. Not many animals grow that fast— it would probably take quite a few years for you to grow a similar amount.

- Crane babies are advanced for their age—they can walk as soon as they hatch out of their eggs, and they're also born with their eyes open. There's a special name for baby animals that can see and walk right away—they're called "precocial."

SO YOU THINK YOU CAN DANCE?

Cranes often dance to impress a mate, pairing up and showing off their best moves. But they don't just dance for romance—they can dance year-round for almost any reason, sometimes in huge groups. Young cranes are taught to dance by their parents, and sometimes they practice their moves for years before whipping them out when they're ready to start a family of their own.

Crane dancing is weird. It can be very elegant, but it can also be downright hilarious. They bob their heads up and down rapidly, leap back and forth, flap their wings, bow toward the ground, and occasionally throw their heads back to make a loud call. They also show off by picking up food or sticks and throwing them high into the air.

CLOUDS OF CRANES

Many cranes spend winter in warmer areas and then fly back to cooler areas in spring to breed. The sight of a whole herd of cranes migrating across the sky is awe-inspiring, although once cranes are up in the air you can't always see them easily—some species can fly as high as 6 miles, which isn't too far off the height a plane flies at!

BIRDS IN DANGER

In 1941 there were only 16 **whooping cranes** left in the world, mostly due to habitat loss and hunting. People have worked hard to save these birds from extinction, and their numbers have grown, but there is still only one flock of these beautiful birds left in the wild.

STANDING OUT

- Aside from the red caps on their heads, **sandhill cranes** are mostly gray all over. That is, until they start to preen with their beaks—their beaks are often coated in mud from searching for food, and it gets rubbed into their feathers until they have a distinctive red or brown tinge to their coat.

- **Gray crowned cranes** don't need mud to stand out—they have a crown-like fan of pale, golden-hued feathers sticking up above their heads like feathered royalty.

CORN-FED CRANES

Cranes often hunt for water-dwelling prey such as fish and frogs, but they also gobble down insects, mice, and even snakes. Plants are on the menu, too—sometimes cranes forage in the wild, and at other times they make use of crops grown by human farmers. **Sandhill cranes** often make a pit stop during their migration, taking a break in Nebraska, to fuel up on corn left on the ground after the fields have been harvested. The cornfields are close to the Platte River, the perfect stopping place for cranes to gather, sleep, and feed, gorging themselves so they'll have energy later on.

OWLS

Because most owls are up and about at night, you might not have had the pleasure of seeing one in the flesh. So you could be surprised to learn just how big some owls can get, or that they have some seriously odd habits—including running along the ground on their huge, scaly feet or collecting their own poop.

WHO'S WHO

There are two distinct kinds of owls: **true owls** and **barn owls** (and their relatives). True owls are a huge group—there are over 220 species, ranging from the huge **Eurasian eagle owl** to the tiny **elf owl**. Barn owls stand out because of their large heads with heart-shaped faces.

A GROUP OF OWLS iS CALLED A PARLiAMENT.

CLIMATE CHANGE

The habitats of some owls, like the alpine grasslands used by **sooty owls** in New Guinea, are being destroyed by climate change. Many owls also need large, old trees with hollows in them in order to nest, so deforestation is leading to habitat loss and making it harder for them to nest.

WHERE CAN I SEE AN OWL?

Owls live on every continent except Antarctica.

HUNTING HABITS

Owls use their powerful hearing to hunt. Some owls can even hear prey as it moves under the cover of dirt, leaves, or snow. When it comes to catching their prey, owls have lots of different techniques.

► Owls often perch on a branch, sometimes staying so still that they look as if they're sleeping. But they're just concentrating! When a suitable meal appears below them, the owl drops swiftly down from the tree to pounce on it.

► Hunting from flight is also a common technique. Huge wings allow owls to glide, and the soft, ragged edges of their wings help them move through the air silently. That means they can sneak up on their prey, swooping in before the poor creature has heard them coming.

► **Fish owls**, as their name suggests, love eating fish, plus other water-dwelling creatures, such as frogs. They often hunt for their prey by perching on a rock in or beside a river, then darting down to grab wriggling fish in their claws as they swim past.

► **Burrowing owls**, who spend a lot of time on the ground, are able to run after their prey! These odd owls also stockpile their poop, stacking it up around their burrows to tempt dung beetles. Once the beetles are lured close enough, the owls snatch them up and eat them.

NIGHT OWLS

Although some owls hunt during the day, most owls sleep when the sun is up. The colors and patterns on their feathers help them blend into their surroundings, which means they don't need to bother finding a place to hide as they sleep in broad daylight—you could walk right past one having a snooze on a branch and not see it.

OWLS EAT MICE, RIGHT?

Owls are carnivores, and they're not picky—some species eat more than 100 different types of prey. The smallest owls often eat insects, but others can hunt animals that are two or three times bigger than them! Common owl foods include mice, rabbits, and small birds, but they also eat a range of much more surprising things, such as koalas, raccoons, eagles, herons, monkeys, skunks, sloth, small deer, baby foxes, warthogs, and even hedgehogs. **OUCH!**

OWL  EYES

OWLS DON'T HAVE PERFECT EYESIGHT, BUT FOR EVERY FLAW THEY HAVE A COOL BONUS FEATURE THAT MAKES THEIR VISION TRULY REMARKABLE.

▶ Owls don't have round eyeballs like yours—theirs are like long tubes. This means their eyeballs can't move around in their sockets to see in different directions very well. To make up for it, they have double the number of vertebrae—the building blocks of bone in the spine—as other birds. That means they can easily turn their heads to look straight behind them.

▶ Owls don't have great color vision, but they can see extra well at night. They can see tiny contrasts between different shades of black and gray, so seeing even the smallest movements in their surroundings is possible on dark, shadowy nights.

▶ Owl eyesight is excellent for things that are far away, but it isn't very good for things that are right in front of them! To help them keep track of things close by, owls have a whole lot of whiskery feathers around their beaks called "filoplumes." These sensitive feathers help them sense things, including their prey, once they are too close to see.

▶ The **great horned owl** has the largest eyes of any owl. If these birds were as big as you, their eyeballs would be as big as oranges!

PUKING PELLETS

Owls often swallow their prey whole, only shredding it into strips if it is particularly large. Eating every part of an animal has an interesting side effect, which is that owls throw up every day, sometimes more than once. They're not doing it because they're sick, though! And their puke isn't gloopy like yours—it's quite a firm pellet, made out of all the little bits of animal that the owl couldn't digest, including fur, bone, and feathers. **ICK!**

TAKING A DIP

Owls can swim, although generally only if they really need to, such as if they accidentally fall into water. As you would imagine, swimming owls look quite awkward! Their heads stick out of the water, buoyed by their outstretched wings. They use their wings like oars to paddle toward land, their bodies bobbing up and down as their wings rotate to propel them forward. They can't take off from the water, so they need to swim to land and dry out their wings before they can get back into the air.

HOME SWEET HOME

▶ Some owls, such as **great horned owls**, take over the nests of birds like ravens and magpies.

▶ **Goggle-eyed Cuban screech owls** make their own nests, hollowing out a little nook in a tree—usually a palm tree!

▶ Some desert-dwelling owls, like **elf owls** and **ferruginous pygmy owls**, raise their owlets (baby owls) in cacti. They use nest holes that were originally hollowed out by woodpeckers.

▶ **Burrowing owls** don't nest in trees—they live in underground burrows. Sometimes they dig their own, but they will also take over burrows created by prairie dogs, armadillos, or ground squirrels.

▶ **Grass owls** only ever nest on the ground. They hollow out grassy tunnels, with a nest formed out of a tussock of grass tucked away in the center.

• FLANNERY FILE •

Powerful owls live in the botanic gardens in Sydney, Australia—it's one of the best places to see them. There are a couple of really big Moreton Bay fig trees in the gardens, and the owls are often perched in them. I once was walking through the botanic gardens and found a pile of possum guts on the ground. I knew what that meant! I looked up into the trees and, sure enough, there was a powerful owl with a ring-tailed possum gripped tightly in its claws. You need to look super carefully if you want to catch a glimpse of an owl. Start by looking on the ground for the leftover parts of their prey—like the wing of a flying fox, or the bones or guts of a possum or a mouse. As they eat, owls often drop little bits of their meal on the ground below. Look up, and don't be discouraged if you can't see anything right away. Eventually you'll probably see a great big feathery owl sitting where the leaves are thickest—you might even spot a whole family!

WHAT A MOUTHFUL!

The largest owl that ever lived, now extinct, was called the ***Ornimegalonyx***—try saying that ten times fast! It lived on the island of Cuba, in the Caribbean. It stood 3.6 feet tall, about the size of a six-year-old child, and weighed at least 19 pounds. It was a hunter, and easily able to kill the young of the giant sloths that are now extinct but once inhabited the island.

SKY • OWLS

31

PELICANS

Nearly everything about a pelican is big—all eight species have large rotund bodies, giant scaly feet, and huge wings. But the most eye-catching body part is doubtlessly their enormous, record-breaking bill! Pelicans can do some seriously cool things with their bills, although fish would probably describe their bills as "terrifying" rather than "cool." It's all about perspective.

STARTING A FAMILY

Pelicans often come together in colonies to lay their eggs, with hundreds or even thousands of birds building nests close together. Both parents share egg-minding duties, often using their large feet to help keep them warm.

LUSCIOUS LOCKS

Dalmatian pelicans sport a crop of long feathers on top of their heads, which often look strangely like a human hairstyle, or even a feathery wig.

A GROUP OF PELICANS iS CALLED A SCOOP.

WHERE CAN I SEE A PELICAN?

Pelicans live on every continent except Antarctica.

DEEP DIVES

Brown pelicans have different eating habits from other pelicans. They fly above water, scouting for food with their keen eyesight. Once they spot a fish they dive toward the water at incredible speeds, slamming into their prey to stun them before gulping them down. All of that hurtling around and smacking into water would hurt a lot of other animals, but these birds have a stack of nifty tricks to stop themselves from getting injured.

▶ Tensing all of their muscles as they dive stops their necks from breaking when they hit the water.

▶ The body parts that help these pelicans to breathe and swallow (the trachea and esophagus) sit on the right side of their necks, so they turn toward the left as they dive to protect these delicate parts from hard collisions with the water.

▶ Inflating special air sacs under their skin helps soften the impact of their landing.

BILL OF CHAMPIONS

▶ Pelicans have the longest bills of any bird in the world, sometimes stretching to nearly 1.5 feet long. The pouch hanging below, referred to as the "gular pouch," is also impressively spacious—it can hold up to 3.5 gallons of water!

▶ **Australian pelican** pouches are usually a combination of soft pinks and yellows, but during breeding season these colors become much brighter and are also joined by splashes of vivid blue. Once the eggs have been laid, the colors tone back down.

▶ **White pelicans**, both male and female, grow a large lump on their beaks during mating season. It looks a bit like a horn and falls off once the eggs have been laid. It's thought that this special beak growth makes the pelicans more attractive to potential mates.

HOW DO YOU IMPRESS A PELICAN?

In breeding season, multiple **Australian pelican** males compete for the attention of a female. A parade of male pelicans follow a female as she walks around, trying to impress her by throwing fish, sticks, and other objects into the air and swinging their bills around. Eventually, the males start to drop off one by one—a bit like contestants being eliminated on a reality TV show—until just one is left.

FLANNERY FILE

I have heard some funny stories about pelicans occasionally eating other birds, and they've apparently even been reported to eat the odd chihuahua! I've seen pelicans going head to head with sea eagles quite a few times. When sea eagles are young, they're very silly—they don't know how to do anything, and they'll have a go at anything. They often learn to fly in the hungry part of the year, when there isn't a lot of food around, so they're always on the lookout for a meal. They'll be flying around, see a flock of pelicans and think, *Oh, they'd be good to eat*. Of course, when they try to take on a pelican, they don't stand a chance! All a pelican has to do is pull its beak open and go "Aarrrrrr!" for the pesky young sea eagle to quickly rethink its plan, turn around, and flee.

WHO'S DOING THE EATING?

Once you know that pelicans sometimes eat meals of the feathered variety, it can be concerning to see a pelican chick ducking its head inside an adult's enormous gaping bill. But don't worry! The chick isn't about to be eaten— it's clambering in to *get* a meal. Chicks can't hunt for themselves, so if they're hungry they snack on regurgitated fish paste from their parents' beaks. DELICIOUS!

GONE FISHIN'

Despite their bills being able to hold more than their stomachs, pelicans don't use them as lunchboxes to store snacks for later—they swallow their food as they catch it. Fresh is best!

▶ Most pelicans hunt by floating on top of the water and dipping their beaks in to find fish. Their bills have a lethal hook at the end that helps them to latch on to even the slipperiest of fish. Once they've caught something, pelicans squeeze the muscles in their bill to empty out all of the water they've scooped up with their prey before swallowing it whole.

▶ Many pelican species hunt and feed in large groups, working together to gang up on their prey. They get into formation, which is often a curved line, then beat their wings on the surface of the water and poke their bills around to herd fish into groups so they can pick them off. Sometimes they even direct the fish toward shallow water, where they're easier to catch.

▶ Pelicans are known for using their size to muscle in and snatch meals from other birds. But pelicans can get robbed, too! Gulls sometimes stand on a pelican's head, waiting until they catch a fish before ducking in to nab the pelican's meal for themselves. **SNEAKY!**

SEE-FOOD DIET

Pelicans are carnivorous, and they're not particularly fussy eaters. They mostly eat fish but will also go after other water-dwelling animals such as yabbies, crayfish, frogs, and turtles. They've even been known to gobble down other birds, including seagulls, ducklings, and pigeons. Because they don't have any teeth, they swallow their prey whole— usually headfirst. **GRUESOME!**

WHO'S BIGGER—YOU OR A PELICAN?

Pelicans are some of the heaviest flying birds in the world. **Dalmatian pelicans** are the largest, sometimes weighing in at nearly 33 pounds. That's over half the weight of a fully grown dalmatian—the dog kind, that is! They can also stand up to 6 feet tall, which is taller than some adult humans (including Beyoncé). Their wingspan is even more impressive, reaching over 10 feet!

HUMMINGBIRDS

Most of the 338 hummingbird species don't sing or hum—they're named after the humming sound their wings make as they move at speeds too fast for your eyes to follow. Many hummingbirds have patches of iridescent feathers on their bodies, earning them the nickname "flying jewels." But they're not just beautiful! Relative to the size of their bodies, hummingbirds have the largest brains of any bird, and the second largest of any animal.

WHERE CAN I SEE A HUMMINGBIRD?

Hummingbirds live right across the Americas, from Alaska down to the very tip of South America. They're particularly common in South America. When people think of hummingbirds, they often imagine them in a rainforest, drinking nectar from an exotic tropical flower. Plenty of hummingbirds do thrive in tropical areas, but they're surprisingly versatile birds. Certain species can be found high up in cool mountainous regions where oxygen is scarce, and even in deserts!

A GROUP OF HUMMINGBIRDS IS CALLED A CHARM.

FLOWER EATERS

HUMMINGBIRDS HAVE SPECIAL BODY PARTS THAT HELP THEM GATHER NECTAR.

Hummingbirds have a very high metabolism—higher than most other animals, including you. That means they burn through energy really quickly and need to eat regularly to keep their strength up. They can eat up to three times their body weight in food each day.

- Each species of hummingbird has a slightly different beak that's perfectly suited to the specific types of flower they like to eat. Some hummingbirds have extra-long beaks so they can reach the nectar at the bottom of long, trumpet-shaped flowers. Beaks can either poke straight out or curve downward to fit the shape of certain flowers, too.

- Hummingbird tongues are often twice as long as their beaks! They're also almost completely clear, with a forked tip a bit like a snake's tongue, and they're hollow, too! Each one has two tubes, and when poked into flowers the tubes fill up with nectar. The tongues don't work like straws, though—hummingbirds can't suck nectar up through them. Instead, they have to pull their tongues inside their mouths to empty each load of nectar, so their tongues are constantly flicking in and out as they eat.

- Hummingbirds are omnivores, so even though nectar makes up most of their diet, they eat things like insects and spiders as well.

- Some hummingbirds can eat nectar from more than 1,000 flowers in a single day. They have excellent memories and are able to keep track of where the best nectar is, returning to those same flowers over and over again.

- Hummingbirds help to pollinate plants—they pick up pollen from flowers as they feed, carrying it to other flowers as they travel to eat. Some plants can only be pollinated by hummingbirds and couldn't survive without them.

CLIMATE CHANGE

Climate change could have a huge impact on hummingbirds by destroying the forests they depend upon.

SKY ● HUMMINGBIRDS

37

FANCY FEATHERS
AND DARING DIVES

> MALE HUMMINGBIRDS OFTEN LOOK EXTRA SPECIAL, WITH BRIGHT PATCHES OF PLUMAGE OR ELABORATE TAIL FEATHERS. THEY USE THEIR FLASHY LOOKS, ALONG WITH IMPRESSIVE ATHLETIC DISPLAYS, TO ATTRACT A MATE.

▶ Many hummingbirds, like **ruby-throated** or **blue-throated hummingbirds**, have patches of vivid color on their throats that appear even brighter in certain lights, so the birds angle themselves to show their feathers off in the best possible way.

▶ Some males can fan out their throat feathers so that they're impossible to miss. The **calliope hummingbird** is one such bird, with beautiful pink neck feathers that can puff out into remarkable spikes.

▶ Some males, including the **marvelous spatuletail**, have very long, hair-like feathers on their tails, each one tipped with a brightly colored fan of feathers. They hover in front of females and wave their tails around to win over their mates.

▶ Both male and female **booted racket-tails** have the added feature of fluffy white feathers clumped around their legs—like teeny tiny boots.

▶ **Anna's** and **Costa's hummingbirds** make a series of outlandish dives to impress their mates, flying up into the air and hurtling down nearly 130 feet before heading back up to do it all over again. The wind moving through their feathers as they plummet downward makes a distinctive chirping sound!

HEADING ON VACATION

Although some hummingbirds stay put over winter, many species travel long distances to escape the cold—chasing after the sun and the flowering plants that supply them with nectar. **Rufous hummingbirds** have the longest journeys—they can travel close to 3,100 miles as they move from their summer home in Alaska to their winter home in Mexico.

FLANNERY FILE

I lived near Boston for a year and was often amazed at the huge "insects" I saw and heard dashing between flowers. It was only when one of them hovered for a moment in front of a bloom that I saw that it was no insect—it was a **ruby-throated hummingbird!**

STARTING A FAMILY

Hummingbirds build cozy nests out of various bits of plant matter. Depending on the type of hummingbird, the shape of the nest varies—some are rounded on the bottom, others are pointed. Sometimes the birds build their nests underneath overhanging leaves so that rain won't fall inside. Egg sizes vary between species, but they all have something in common— they're tiny!

A BIRD OR A BEE?

Hummingbirds are the smallest birds in the world. Their scientific name is Trochilidae—Greek for "small bird." The tiniest of them all is the **bee hummingbird**, which weighs a measly 0.06 ounces, about the same as a playing card. They can also be under 2 inches long—that's only a little longer than an Oreo! These bright green birds live in Cuba, where they're called "zunzuncito" because of the humming "zun zun" sound they make as they fly. Even the biggest hummingbirds are still quite small. The **giant hummingbird** might be giant compared with the bee hummingbird, but it's still only about 8 inches long, or the length of a large banana.

THE SMALLEST HUMMINGBIRD EGGS CAN BE AS SMALL AS TIC TACS.

SHAKE IT OFF

When hummingbirds get caught in the rain and need to dry off, they act a bit like a dog—shaking their head and body vigorously to send droplets of water flying. They twist their heads so violently during this process that their necks turn almost 90 degrees!

WING MASTERS

When it comes to flying, hummingbirds are unlike any other bird.

▶ Hummingbirds don't just flap their wings up and down; they make a complex rotating movement that gives them extra power. The chest muscles that make their wings move are so big they make up about 30 percent of their entire body mass.

▶ They can fly backward and even upside down!

▶ Hummingbirds are the only birds that can hover in the exact same place for more than 30 seconds—in fact, they can do this for minutes at a time!

▶ The fastest a hummingbird's wings can move is about 100 beats per second—so fast that their wings are just a blur.

OXPECKERS

You can get a lot of clues about what oxpeckers are like from their name—these birds are often found on large animals, including oxen, and they love to peck! Their scientific name, *Buphagus*, means "eater of cattle," which is slightly misleading—these tiny birds aren't exactly capable of devouring a cow! But the things they eat are still shocking in their own way . . .

WHERE CAN I SEE AN OXPECKER?

Oxpeckers are found only in Africa, where there are lots of large mammals to peck at and live on.

EXTREME NAPPING

Oxpeckers occasionally take naps on their hosts during daylight hours, holding tight as their hosts move around. Sometimes they even settle in and sleep, clinging to their hosts overnight.

A GROUP OF OXPECKERS IS CALLED A FLING.

STAY BACK!

Oxpeckers hiss when they're feeling threatened, which can be a helpful warning for their host animal that there might be danger nearby.

WHAT DOES AN OXPECKER LOOK LIKE?

There are two different species of oxpecker—**red-billed** and **yellow-billed**. Red-billed oxpeckers do indeed have red bills. Yellow-billed oxpeckers' bills are vivid yellow at the base, with bright red tips.

WHAT KIND OF FOOD CAN YOU FIND ON A GIRAFFE?

Oxpeckers cling on to their hosts and eat any insects they find. They eat a lot of different insects, including flies, maggots, and fleas, and they particularly love gobbling down ticks. The reason oxpeckers love ticks so much is that their real favorite food is blood. Ticks burrow into the host animal's skin so that they can drink its blood, and by the time the oxpeckers pluck them out they're like the bug version of a jam doughnut—crisp on the outside and full of oozy red blood in the center. Delicious! Blood isn't the only bodily fluid oxpeckers eat—they also happily suck down snot, spit, tears, and eye goo. Other less-than-appetizing snacks include dandruff and earwax. **EWW!**

AN UNCONVENTIONAL HOUSE

Oxpeckers spend most of their time hanging out with much larger animals. They like to perch on animals such as cattle, giraffes, rhinos, zebras, water buffalo, hippos, and antelope, and they particularly like hairy animals. Using their strong feet and sharp claws, these tenacious little birds can hold on just about anywhere, staying balanced at amazing angles.

Some animals, like elephants, don't particularly like oxpeckers buzzing around—just as you might wave away a fly that was trying to land on you, elephants will often shake off these birds.

CAN YOU LIVE YOUR WHOLE LIFE ON A WILDEBEEST?

Although oxpeckers can eat, sleep, play, and even mate on their hosts, there are times when they have no choice but to leave. For starters, there isn't any water on a host (none that is salt-free, anyway—tears don't count!), so thirsty oxpeckers have to leave. It's also really impractical to lay eggs on a moving animal. They'd just roll right off! Oxpeckers find holes in trees to nest in, lining them with grass and feathers, as well as hair that the birds have plucked right out of their host animal's skin.

WOODPECKERS

Woodpeckers are part of a family of birds called Picidae. They're famous for drilling holes into wood with fierce determination, but wood isn't the only surface at risk of being obliterated by their sharp beaks! It might seem, at first glance, that they're incredibly destructive birds, but woodpeckers can actually make trees healthier by drilling in and removing the pesky insects that are boring into the wood and hurting the tree. All of the birds in the Picidae family are called "woodpeckers," but some of them also have other names, such as **sapsuckers**, **piculets**, and **wrynecks**.

A GROUP OF WOODPECKERS IS CALLED A DESCENT, BUT A GROUP OF SAPSUCKERS IS SOMETIMES CALLED A SLURP.

WHERE CAN I SEE A WOODPECKER?

Woodpeckers don't live in Australia, New Zealand, New Guinea, Madagascar, or the polar regions, but they live just about everywhere else. They're particularly common in the Americas and Southeast Asia.

ALL KINDS OF SNACKS

Most woodpeckers eat lots of insects—they peck holes into trees with their sharp beaks so that they can gobble up the little critters living under the bark or inside the wood. But woodpeckers are a versatile bunch, and other types of food are often on the menu, too.

▶ Plenty of woodpeckers eat sap every now and then, but the woodpeckers known as **sapsuckers** are particularly mad about it. They drill lots of small holes into trees to get to the sap flowing below, which sometimes creates a spotty pattern on the tree's bark. They don't actually suck the sap through their beaks —they lick it up with their tongues.

▶ **Gila woodpeckers**, along with some of their close relatives,

have been recorded using their sharp beaks to crack open the skulls of other birds' nestlings so they can eat the blood and brains inside.

▶ Some **golden-fronted woodpeckers** eat so much of the prickly pears growing on cacti that their little faces go purple from the juice.

▶ **Acorn woodpeckers** eat—you guessed it—acorns! They hide their food for later by pecking acorn-sized holes in trees and squeezing a single acorn into each one. Sometimes acorn woodpeckers can pack 50,000 nuts in a single tree, each one in its own little hole! Sometimes they find other places to drill into and hide acorns—like telephone poles, fence posts, or even wooden houses!

LIVING IN A TREE HOUSE

Woodpecker parents often drill holes into trees to nest in, but **bamboo woodpeckers** drill their nests into bamboo, and some desert-dwelling woodpeckers, like **gila woodpeckers** and **ladder-backed woodpeckers**, hollow out nesting holes in cactus plants! Some ground-dwelling woodpeckers, like the **Andean flicker**, dig hollows into the ground to nest in, and **campo flickers** will occasionally build their nests directly into termite mounds.

EXPERT TREE CLIMBERS

Most woodpeckers spend a lot of time in trees, hunting for food. Their sharp claws grip onto the bark, allowing them to walk up and down vertical surfaces such as tree trunks. Many species have particularly stiff tail feathers that help them balance against the tree, kind of like an extra leg. These feathers have sharp, spiky ends that can grip onto bark, too. **HANDY!**

HOW BIG IS A WOODPECKER?

One of the largest woodpeckers is the **great slaty woodpecker**, which can grow to just over 20 inches tall. **Piculets** are the smallest of the woodpeckers, sometimes measuring less than 3 inches. They don't have the long, stiff tails that many other woodpecker species have—some barely have a tail at all!

CRITTER CATCHERS AND SAP SLURPERS

Woodpeckers have very long, agile tongues that can snake into freshly drilled crevices and holes to latch on to insects or sap. Woodpecker tongues aren't just attached inside their mouths like human tongues are—they wrap right around their skulls like an elastic band holding a lunchbox closed. Tongues can also be up to 4 inches long in some birds! Different woodpecker species have their own style of tongue, each one perfect for eating the particular kind of food they enjoy.

▸ **Sapsuckers** and other sap eaters have an oddly hairy tongue, a bit like a little brush, which helps mop up liquid foods.

▸ Woodpeckers that tunnel into wood for things like insect larvae often have a tongue with a barbed tip that helps catch onto their prey.

▸ Species of woodpeckers that forage on the ground for things like ants, like the **northern flicker**, have tongues with flat tips that help scoop up their food as it tries to scurry away.

DO WOODPECKERS EAT WOOD?

Woodpeckers don't eat the wood they excavate—in fact, they have some special features that stop woodchips or dust from getting inside their bodies.

▸ Woodpeckers have an extra eyelid on each eye that helps keep their eyeballs safe from flying debris, a bit like a carpenter wearing safety glasses while working. These eyelids have the added bonus of helping to keep the bird's eyeballs from bursting or popping out when they're drilling!

▸ Groups of bristly feathers near woodpeckers' nostrils keep wood shavings from getting caught inside the nostrils and blocking them up.

I'M WITH THE
BAND

Sometimes, woodpeckers peck at wood not because they're nesting or finding food—they just want to make a loud noise! Males are the most likely to drum, and each one has his own distinct style, just like human musicians do. This drumming behavior can help attract a mate, or warn off interlopers in their territory.

PROTECT YOUR HEAD

Woodpeckers can peck over 20 times in a single second, and sometimes over 10,000 times in the course of a day. Just thinking about that is enough to give humans a headache, so how do these birds do it day after day?

▶ Woodpecker skulls are very solid on the outside, but they have a thick, spongy layer of bone underneath the hard outer layer. This porous buffer helps absorb the impact of all that pecking before it makes it to the bird's brain.

▶ There is a lot of muscle built up around woodpeckers' necks, which helps stop their spines from getting hurt as they ricochet back and forth.

▶ Woodpecker brains are small, held snugly inside their skulls, and angled so that a flattened area faces the front. This flat area helps distribute the shocks across a wider surface.

▶ When they're drilling into a tree, woodpeckers move really quickly. Their beaks are actually only touching the tree for a millisecond or less with each hit, and this shorter period of contact helps keep their brains from being injured.

BIRD OR SNAKE?

When **Eurasian wrynecks** are feeling threatened they make a hissing noise, a bit like a snake, to scare away predators. That's not their only strange skill—they can also turn their remarkably flexible necks 180 degrees to look straight behind them, which is how they got their name.

GLOSSARY

APEX PREDATOR

Apex predators are also called alpha predators or top predators. They are on the top of the food chain, which means that they have no natural predators to fear. They play an important role in maintaining a balanced and healthy ecosystem.

ATMOSPHERE

Atmosphere is the gases surrounding a planet, held there by the planet's gravity. Earth's atmosphere is a very thin layer of air between the earth's surface and the edge of space.

BACTERIA

Bacteria are microscopic single-celled organisms. They can be found in many different places: in the soil, air, and water, as well as on and inside plants and animals—including humans. Some bacteria are beneficial to us, whereas others are destructive.

BIOLUMINESCENCE

Bioluminescence is the production of light by a living organism. This glowing light is created by chemical reactions inside animals' bodies, and can be helpful in many different ways, from scaring off predators to finding food or a mate.

BLOOD CELLS

Blood is made up of blood cells, plus a liquid element called plasma. There are three kinds of blood cells: 1. red blood cells absorb oxygen from the lungs and transport it around the body, 2. white blood cells fight against disease and infection, 3. platelets help to clot the blood and heal wounds.

CARBON

Carbon is a chemical element. It is one of the building blocks that plants and animals are made from, making it essential to all life on Earth. All organic compounds are considered "carbon-based." Carbon can combine with other elements to make new compounds.

CARBON DIOXIDE

Carbon dioxide is a compound made up of one carbon atom (C) and two oxygen atoms (O_2). It is a greenhouse gas, which means it traps the sun's heat close to the earth instead of allowing it to move out into space. Too much carbon dioxide causes the earth to overheat and, as the weather changes, many plants and animals are negatively affected. This is called global warming, or climate change.

CARBON EMISSIONS

When we burn carbon-rich fossil fuels, we release a huge amount of carbon into the air. The carbon then bonds with oxygen to produce carbon dioxide. Over time, the amount of carbon in the atmosphere has risen drastically due to the increased use of fossil fuels.

CARNIVORE/ CARNIVOROUS

Carnivores are animals that exclusively or primarily eat meat—either by killing their meal or by scavenging carcasses.

COLD-BLOODED AND WARM-BLOODED ANIMALS

Warm-blooded animals, or endotherms, use their metabolism to generate the right amount of heat to keep their bodies at the right temperature. Cold-blooded animals, or ectotherms, aren't able to control their body temperature using their metabolism. On cold days, their metabolism drops along with their body temperature, which slows down their physical movement. Endotherms generally need a steady food supply to keep their metabolism generating heat, while ectotherms can often survive long periods without food, thanks to their ability to slow their bodies down and wait out the colder months.

COLONIZATION

In zoology, colonization is when animals or plants move into a new habitat and make it their home.

COLONY

In zoology, a colony is a group of animals or plants of the same kind that live together, and often rely on each other to survive.

CONTINENTS

A continent is a large landmass, and one continent often includes multiple countries. The continents of the world are Europe, Asia, Africa, North and South America, Australia, and Antarctica.

DEFORESTATION

Deforestation is the permanent destruction of forests. People clear the land to graze farmed animals such as cattle, as well as to build or to harvest wood any other tree products (such as palm oil). Deforestation causes habitat loss for many animals and can lead to the extinction of species that need the forest to survive. It also reduces the number of trees taking CO_2 out of the atmosphere, which means that our atmosphere fills up with more greenhouse gas emissions.

DOMESTICATED SPECIES

Domesticated species are animals that have been bred to benefit humans, often over many generations. Animals are often domesticated so that humans can use parts of their bodies (such as flesh, skin, fur, or bone), or things that they produce (such as milk or eggs), for food, clothing, and decoration. Animals are also often domesticated to use as labor or to keep as pets.

DROUGHT

Drought is a prolonged period with much less rainfall than usual, or no rainfall at all. Drought causes rivers and lakes to dry up, which leaves many animals without water to drink. It causes plants to die, which can result in habitat loss and less food for animals to eat. Many animal populations are threatened by drought, and climate change is increasing the instances of drought around the world.

ECHOLOCATION

Echolocation is the use of echoes and soundwaves to find out where an object is in space. Many animals use echolocation to hunt and navigate, like dolphins, whales, bats, and some bird species.

ECOSYSTEM

An ecosystem is a finely balanced environment, in which all the living things (plants, animals and other organisms) and nonliving things (like rocks and the weather) work together to maintain the system's health.

FERAL ANIMALS

Feral animals are domesticated animals that have been released into the wild and continued to reproduce there—for example, feral cats, goats, camels, and dogs. Feral animals can often endanger the lives of wild animals by preying on them.

FORAGING

When an animal searches for food in the wild, this is called foraging.

FOSSIL FUELS

Fossil fuels are made from fossilized plants and animals that have been buried under the soil for millions of years. Fossil fuels include things like oil, coal, and natural gas.

GENES

Genes are made up of DNA, and they're the things that make each animal in the world unique. They exist inside the cells of living things, like plants and animals, and are passed on from parents to their offspring. In humans, the combination of genes passed on by both parents can determine the appearance of their child, through things such as eye or hair color.

GREENHOUSE GAS EMISSIONS

Greenhouse gases absorb the heat that radiates off the earth's surface and bounce it back, trapping heat in the atmosphere rather than releasing it into space. The main greenhouse gases are water vapor, carbon dioxide, methane, and nitrous oxide. Fossil fuels are the biggest human cause of greenhouse gas emissions.

HERBIVORE/ HERBIVOROUS

Herbivores are animals that have an exclusively or primarily plant-based diet.

HORMONES

Hormones are chemicals inside plants and animals that help all of these living things to function. In plants, hormones help to control growth, as well as the production of flowers or fruit. In animals, hormones are used to send messages to different parts of the body to help it operate. Hormones affect all sorts of things, like growth, sleep, temperature, hunger, and much more.

HUNTING

For animals, hunting is the activity of killing and eating other animals. For humans, hunting also includes killing animals, but not always for food.

INCUBATION

Incubation is the process of keeping eggs at the right temperature while embryos grow inside them. Different animals incubate their eggs in different ways, such as sitting on them or burying them in sand, dirt, or plant matter.

INVERTEBRATE

Invertebrates lack a backbone; they either have a gooey, spongy body (like jellyfish and worms) or they have an exoskeleton (like insects and crabs).

KERATIN

Keratin is a strong, fibrous protein. It is the main substance that forms body parts like hair, nails, hoofs, horns, feathers, and the outermost layers of skin and scales.

LARVAE

Many animals begin their life as larvae before eventually growing into their adult form. Larvae generally look completely different from their parents, and often need very different conditions to survive. For example, tadpoles are the larvae of frogs, and caterpillars are the larvae of butterflies.

MAMMALS

Mammals are a very broad class of animals. Some walk, some swim, and some fly, and their diets can vary from carnivorous to herbivorous, but they all have a number of traits in common, including that they have hair or fur, feed their young with milk, and are warm-blooded.

MARSUPIALS

Marsupials are a group of mammals. Most female marsupials have a pouch where they keep their babies when they're very young, so that they can continue to grow and develop in a safe, warm place. Some marsupial species are herbivores, others are carnivores, and there are also some omnivorous species. Most of the world's marsupials live in Australia and South America.

MEMBRANES

A membrane is a thin layer of tissue. Membranes can be found inside all living things—each cell inside a plant or animal is surrounded by a membrane—but membranes can also be found in many other places. Some animals are born completely surrounded by a membrane, which they then break out of, and other animals have protective membranes underneath their eyelids that help keep their eyes safe.

METABOLISM

Metabolism refers to the chemical reactions that happen inside an organism to keep it alive. There are many different metabolic reactions, but the main ones involve releasing energy or using energy. For example, an animal's metabolism digests the food it eats and converts that food into a form that can be released as energy. Animals also use their energy to grow and repair their bodies.

MIGRATION

Migration is a movement from one place to another. Animals often migrate each year at about the same time, and different species migrate for different reasons. Migrations commonly occur as animals travel to places where food is more plentiful, or the weather is better, or to places where they can find a mate or breed.

NOCTURNAL

Nocturnal animals are active during the night and rest during the day.

OMNIVORE/OMNIVOROUS

Omnivores are animals that eat a variety of meat and plant matter.

ORGANISM

An organism is an animal, a plant or a single-celled life form.

OXYGEN

Oxygen is a gas that makes up part of the air we breathe. It's highly reactive, which means it bonds easily with other elements (for example, carbon). Animals rely on oxygen to survive—they breathe it in and use it to convert nutrients into energy, releasing carbon dioxide as a waste product of this process. Plants exist in perfect symbiosis with animals, as they absorb carbon dioxide and release oxygen.

PARASITE

A parasite is an organism that makes its home in or on an organism of another species, relying on it for food, shelter, and everything else it needs to live. The organism that a parasite makes its home on is called its "host."

PECTINES

Pectines are comb-like structures found on many animals. They can be used for many different things, including grooming, filtering food, and as a sense organ to help the animals feel their surroundings.

PHEROMONES

Pheromones are a type of hormone—a chemical that some animals release to communicate with other members of their species. Pheromones can be released for many reasons, including to attract a mate, to mark pathways leading to home or food, and even as a warning sign.

PIGMENT

Pigments are colored chemicals in the tissues of animals. Some animals produce their own pigments, whereas others get them from their food.

POACHING

Animal poaching is the illegal capturing or killing of animals.

POLLINATION

Pollination is the way that plants reproduce to create seeds and fruits. Pollination involves the movement of pollen from the male part of a flower (the anther) to the female part (the stigma). Some plants self-pollinate, meaning that the transfer of pollen happens within a single flower, or between different flowers on the same plant. The other form of pollination is cross-pollination, where pollen travels between different plants. Things like wind and water can help pollen to travel between plants, but many plants rely on "pollinators"—animals such as birds and insects—to transfer their pollen.

POLLUTION

Pollution is the introduction of harmful materials or substances into our environment. The three main types of pollution are water, air, and land pollution.

Some examples of pollutants are microplastics in the ocean, greenhouse gas emissions in the atmosphere, and pesticides used in agriculture.

PREDATOR

In zoology, "predator" usually refers to an animal that hunts other animals for food. Parasites are also a kind of predator. Predators are essential to a balanced ecosystem.

PROBOSCIS

A proboscis is a long, flexible snout or feeding organ. Many insects use a proboscis to eat, like some moths and butterflies, but larger animal species can also have a proboscis—like elephants and solenodons.

SANCTUARY

A wildlife sanctuary is a carefully designed environment where endangered wild species are brought to live and be protected from human threats, such as poaching. Proper sanctuaries are as much like the animals' natural

habitats as possible: they have the right climate, and contain the right variety of plant and animal species.

TERRITORY

An animal's territory is the area of land or water that it lives in, claims as its own and defends against trespassers.

TIDE

The tide is the periodic rise and fall of the ocean. Changes in the tide are caused by the earth spinning around, and by the gravitational pull of the sun and the moon.

VERTEBRATE

Vertebrates are animals that have a spine and a well-developed skeleton inside their bodies.

WILD SPECIES

Wild species are animals that have evolved without human interference and live and reproduce independently from humans.

INDEX

ACKNOWLEDGMENTS

I'd like to thank Jane Novak for suggesting this project to me, and the fantastic team at Hardie Grant Egmont, especially Ella Meave. Without their dedication, this book would never have seen the light of day. I'd also like to thank Sam Caldwell for his brilliant illustrations, and Pooja Desai and Kristy Lund-White for their magnificent design work. I owe much gratitude to my wife Kate Holden and our son Coleby. They put up with long absences as I wrote this book. Many colleagues helped me with information, among whom Kris Helgen and Luigi Boitani deserve special mention.